APPLE WATCH 5

BEGINNERS TO ADVANCED

USER'S GUIDE

The complete beginner to expert guide to mastering the features of Apple Watch 5, and troubleshoot common problems.

NEWEL

GOMAN

Copyright

All rights reserved. No part of this publication **Apple Watch 5 Beginners to Advanced User's Guide** may be reproduced, stored in a retrieval system or transmitted in any form or by any means, electronic, mechanical, photocopying, recording, and scanning without permission in writing by the author.

Printed in the United States of America
© 2020 by Newel Goman

Dorween Publishing House
USA | UK | CANADA

About the Author

Newel Goman is a seasoned tech enthusiast with over 17 years of experience in the ICT industry. He has passionately followed and reviewed advancement in tech over the years. He enjoys figuring out how to simplify complex problems. Newel, holds a Bachelor and a Master's Degree in Computer Science and Information Communication Technology, respectively, from Princeton University.

Table of Contents

Copyright ii

About the Author iii

Chapter 1 8

Introduction 8

Hardware Specifications 9

Unboxing your Apple watch series 5 10

Chapter 2 12

Basic operation of the apple watch series 5 12

How to turn on your apple watch 12

How to power off your apple watch 12

The apple watch Digital crown 13

The side button 13

The Speaker 14

The screen 14

The Heart Rate Sensors 14

How to take off your watch bands 15

Charging your Apple watch 16

Chapter 3 17

My Watch App... 17

My watch Menu Features 18

- **App Layout**..18
- **Airplane Mode** 18
- **Apple Watch** 19
- **Notifications** 19
- **Glances** 19
- **Do Not Disturb** 19
- **General** 19
  - **Software updates**..19
  - **Automatic Downloads** 20
  - **Watch Orientation**......................................20
  - **Accessibility** 20
  - **Language & Region** 20
  - **Enable Handoff**..20
  - **Usage** 21
  - **Reset**..21
- **Brightness and Text Size**............................21

- **Sounds & Haptics** 21
- **Passcode** 21
- **Health** 21
- **Privacy** 21
- **Activity** 21
- **Workout** 22

Chapter 4 23

Tips, Tricks, and Hidden Features 23

Always-on display feature 23

How to turn off Always-on display feature 23

How to increase and decrease the brightness of your Apple watch 26

How to change text size 27

How to use the compass 27

How to get notification of the time every 15 minutes, 30 minutes or 1 hour 28

How to use fall detection 30

How to delete apps 31

How to quickly mute your series 5 watch by covering with your palm 32

Hear your watch speak the time 33

The Calculator 34

How to ascertain the stability of any object 35

How to automatically unlock your watch with your iPhone 35

How to find your phone with your Apple watch series 5 36

How to take screenshots on your watch 37

How to use voice memos 38

How to use the weather app 39

How to re-arrange the layout 39

How to find recently opened apps on your Apple watch series 5 40

Measure sound in your area 40

How to change your watch faces 40

How to force restart 41

How to use the theatre mode 41

How to protect your phone from water 42

How to add default responses 43

How to add contacts to Emergency SOS 44

How to set a photo as your watch face 47

How to send messages 47

How to use the night stand clock 48

How to use your apple watch series 5 as a Walkie Talkie
.... 49

How to connect to a Wi-Fi network on your watch 50

Listen to podcasts on your apple watch 51

How to turn your apple watch into a flash light 51

How to check your storage capacity 52

How to place a call on hold 53

How to select apps to get notifications from on your watch 54

How to connect your apple watch to your iPhone 54

Chapter 5 57

Features and Settings 57

Homescreen 57

How to view your battery percentage 57

Power reserve 58

How to customize your watch faces 58

Responding to E-mails 59

Answering phone calls 59

How to transfer calls 60

Access keypad 60

Glances 61

Alarms, Timers, world clock and stop watch 61

Alarms 61

Timer 62

Stop watch 62

Track health and fitness 62

Apple pay and pass book 63

Maps on the apple watch 64

Remote control 64

Stocks 64

How to download third party app on your watch 64

    Chapter 6 66

    Siri 66

    Chapter 7 74

Master The Electrocardiodiagram (ECG) on Apple Watch Series 5 74

    The Apple watch series 5 ECG 78

Chapter 8 81

Trouble shooting Apple watch series 5 81

When your watch gets stuck on the Apple logo 81

Tracking problem with GPS location when working out 81

When activity does not track accurately 82

When Apple watch does not connect in a cellular way from the iPhone 83

When you do not receive a feedback from Siri 83

When the Walkie Talkie is not working 83

When you cannot get notifications for messages and E-mails 84

Chapter 9 86

Essential Apps for Apple Watch Series 5 86

Chapter 1

Introduction

The Apple Watch Series 5 comes fully loaded with amazing features, designed to enhance the health, productivity, and activity of the end-users. Do you want to remain active throughout the day? Or are you looking for ways to track and improve your workout sessions or become more committed to keeping your performance schedule? The good news is that the Apple Watch 5 series has the capability of helping you achieve your set goals with an all-day advanced fitness tracker. You can track a broader range of activities, as it collects a significantly more significant amount of data and gives you a complete picture of your day-to-day activities, not just the quality but also the frequency of your movement.

The Apple watch series 5 has an in-built accelerometer which accurately measures your total body movement. It also has a custom sensor which is designed to measure intensity, as it tracks the rate of your beat. If you have always loved using GPS, then you can get the best out of it on your Apple watch series 5, as it uses the GPS and iPhone to keep track of real-time activities. Over time, your Apple watch would know you, just as a personal trainer, would, by delivering apt reminders, suggest goals and enhances your chances of achieving your daily fitness goals. The Apple watch series 5 also has an in-built pressure sensitivity, which is also called *Force touch*. The starting price for Apple Watch Series 5 is pegged at $399 for the 40mm version.

Hardware Specifications

The Apple watch series 5 appears identical to the series 4 model not only in terms of looks but also with several features. One of the significant differences between the Apple watch series 4 and 5 models is in their storage capacities. The series 4 has a storage capacity of 16GB, while the series 5 has a 32GB storage capacity. However, the most significant difference between series 4 and 5 is the newly introduced *Always-on display feature*. The *Always-on display* feature always leaves your clock on display, unlike the series 4, where you still have to turn your wrist to view the clock. The series 5 also has a 64bit dual-core processor, a magnetometer w/compass, and a new titanium case finishes. With the LTPO OLED retina display, the refresh rate can go from 60Hz to 1Hz. The battery life of series 5 is the same as that of series 4, which lasts for up to about 18hours.

Unboxing your Apple watch series 5

As in the case of other previous models of Apple watches, the Apple watch series 5 comes in a unified design package, where there is a separate package for the watch bands.

Inside the Apple watch series 5 pack includes:
- A 5 watts wall power adapter
- An apple watch magnetic inductive charging cable
- A series 5 watch wrapped in a microfiber pouch
- Apple watch wrist band
- A quick guide

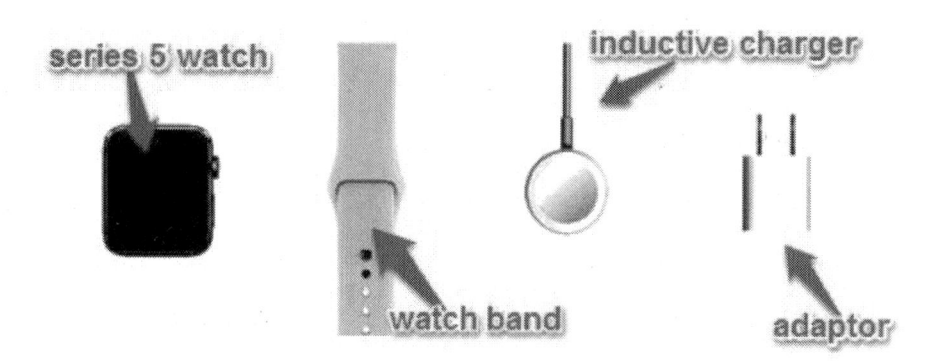

Inside the Apple watch series 5 pack

Series 5 watch unwrapped   *Series 5 watch in a micro fiber pouch*

Chapter 2

Basic operation of the apple watch series 5

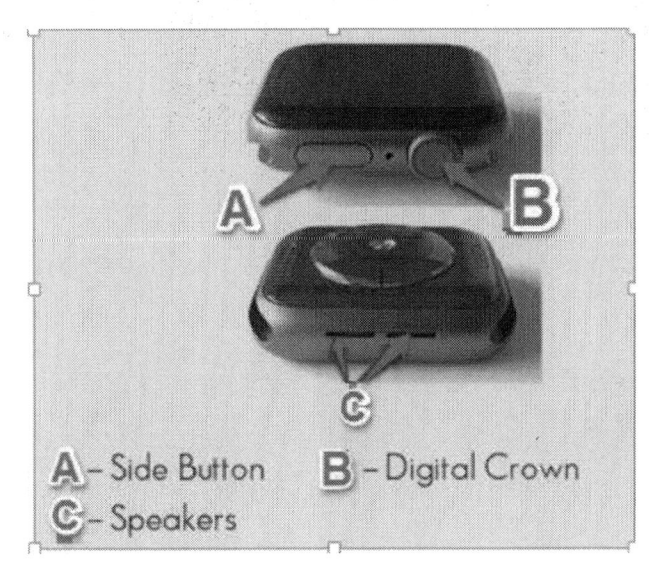

A - Side Button   B - Digital Crown
C - Speakers

How to turn on your apple watch

When the apple watch is powered off, you can power it back on by pressing and holding the side button. You will see the Apple logo coming on, which indicates that the watch is turning on.

How to power off your apple watch

To power off your apple watch, you press and hold the side button, and slide the power off toggle.

The apple watch Digital crown

The digital crown is the small button by the side of your watch. It enables you to scroll and zoom in using the slider on the side. It also serves as a home button when you press it. The home button, when pressed, takes you to the main area, where you will see all the apps. When you press it again, it takes you back to the clock face.

When you double-tap the digital crown, your watch displays the previous application you opened.

When you press and hold *the digital crown*, you will activate Siri.

The side button

One press on the side button will bring out your favorite contacts. You can scroll through them with your digital crown to contact them individually. When you select one of the contacts, you can either call, send a message or pictures, if they have an apple watch as well.

If you double-tap the side button, you can access apple pay.

Pressing and holding the side button will display the menu that will enable you power off your device.

The Speaker

The apple watch series 5 has its speaker on the left side of the watch. The speaker of the series 5 provides an excellent audio sound for a Siri feedback and every two-way communication on your watch.

The screen

The Apple watch series 5 has a touch screen that aids interaction. The display allows you to access all the different settings menu, as it responds to *forced touch'*. The *forced touch* is when you press and hold firmly to the screen of your watch.

The Heart Rate Sensors

The Heart Rate Sensor is another great feature of the Apple watch. You will find the heart rate sensors beneath the apple watch. The heart rate sensors monitor your heart rate as you perform your exercises.

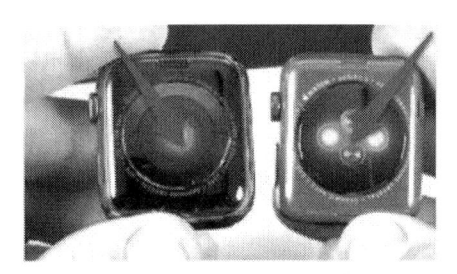

Heart Rate Sensors

How to take off your watch bands

The apple watch series 5 comes with different detachable bands colors. There are two little buttons behind your watch. You can pull out the watch bands when you press in on the little buttons and pulling out the band from side to side. You can also easily slide it back in following same process.

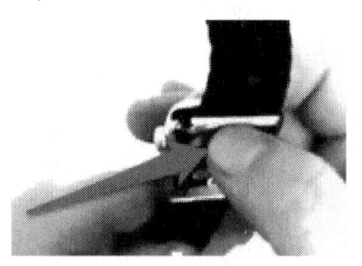

Press the button beneath the watch

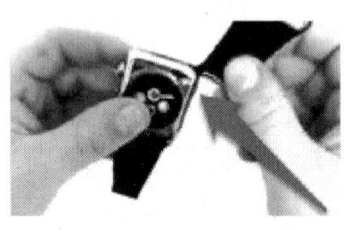

Disengage the band

Removed watch bands

Charging your Apple watch

you can charge your apple watch by placing the charging terminal at the back of your watch, while the othe other end is connected to a wall adapter.

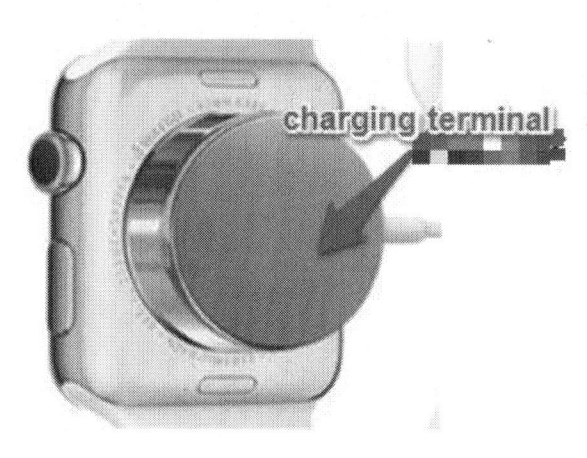

Chapter 3

My Watch App

Your iPhone is synchronised to your Apple watch using the *My Watch* App which should be installed on your iPhone. The synchronization is what enables the settings carried out on your iPhone using the *My Watch* app to reflect on your Apple watch and vice-versa.

When you Launch the *My Watch* app, you will find several features on the menu. These feaatures include: *Do not disturb, Apple watch Notifications, App Layout, Airplane mode, General. Etc*

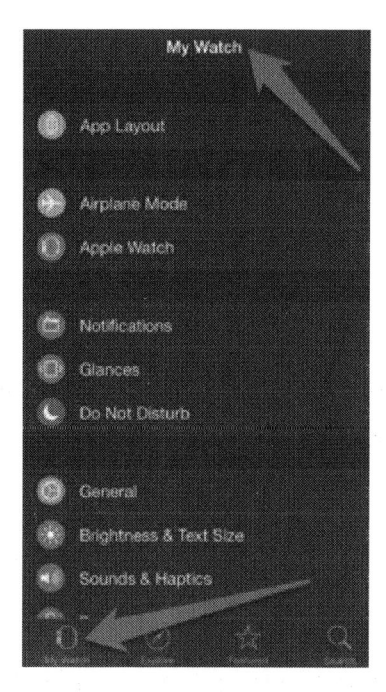

My Watch Menu

My watch Menu Features

- **App Layout:** When you tap on *App Layout,* you get to move any of the installed app icons to wherever you want them to be on the screen. As you position the icons on your iPhone, it also takes effect on your Apple watch.
- **Airplane Mode:** When you tap on the *Airplane Mode,* your phone gets mirrored in terms of airplane mode.

- **Apple Watch:** When you tap on the *Apple Watch,* you get information about the paired apple watch and it also enables you to either pair or unpair your phone to your Apple watch.
- **Notifications:** When you tap on *Notifications*, you get to either activate or de-activate the notifications on your apple watch. You could also select the notifications you would love to appear on your watch. The *Notification privacy* would make the notifications details displayed are limited, hence protecting your privacy.
- **Glances:** You use Glances to easily access your apps. It provides a shortcut a variety of apps. To access Glance, swipe up the clock face of the apple watch, all the apps that have been added to Glances will be displayed. You can also view all the other applications that are compatible with your apple watch. To add to your apple watch list of Glances tap on *plus+* to remove an app from the list of Glances tap on *minus* –
- **Do Not Disturb:** This enables you to *turn On* or *turn Off* the *Do not disturb feature* on your iPhone and Apple watch.

- **General:** When you tap on *General,* you will find other sub-settings. some of the subsettings include:

	- **Software updates:** This enables you to carry out the latest software updates

- **Automatic Downloads***:* This enables compatible apps present on your iPhone to automatically get downloaded on your Apple watch. it displayson the homescreen of your watch after download. You have to turn On automatic downloads to enable it or turn it Off, if you don't like it.
- **Watch Orientation***:* This enables you choos the orientation of the watch face to be synchronized to your preferred wrist. You can choose either your left or right wrist.
- **Accessibility***:* This setting enables you to view voiceover, zoom, grayscale, bold text, reduce motion, reduce transparency, turn labels ON/OFF, accessibility shortcut. To access any of the aforementioned features, you have to toggle on the ones you prefer.
- **Language & Region***:* This is where you can make changes to your language and your region
- **Enable Handoff***:* when you toggle on this feature, it enables you open whatever app

you have on the apple watch on your iPhone.
- **Usage***:* This contains information of how much memory is consumed by the different apps on your apple watch and also tells what your storage capacity is.
- **Reset***:* This enables you to reset your watch.

- **Brightness and Text Size:** This allows you to adjust the screen brightness, as well as text size that is displayed on your apple watch.
- **Sounds & Haptics:** This allows you to increase and decrease sound level. You can also mute sound and increase or decrease Haptic strength.
- **Passcode:** This prevents unauthorized persons from accessing the features of your watch. To activate this feature, turn it on and set up your passcode.
- **Health:** This is where you input all your health information, which becomes very useful for ECG.
- **Privacy:** This enables Apple to track all your activities on the watch.
- **Activity:** You would be able to either activate or de activate different activities carried out on the watch.

- **Workout:** This enables you to select your prefereed workout structure from a list of favourite activities and then set a goal based on how long your exercise will last, as well as, the number of calories you intend to burn or how far you want to go. The glance feature shows you how fast, how long and how far your progress is. You can see the summary of your workout session when you are done and also win awards for your level of achievement. All your workout data and history is stored on the Fitness App on your iPhone stores, making it easy to keep track of your progress. Your data also gets shared with any third party health and fitness app also.

Chapter 4

Tips, Tricks, and Hidden Features

Always-on display feature

This is a new and one of the most prominent features that come with iPhone watch series 5. When you are not twisting your wrist or tapping the screen of your watch, the clock will always be on display, unlike the series 4 model, which responds only when you turn your wrist or tap the screen.

How to turn off Always-on display feature

You can turn off the *Always-on display feature,* if you do not want your time to always be on display

Step 1: Tap on the watch app on your iPhone.

Step 2: tap on *Display and Brightness*

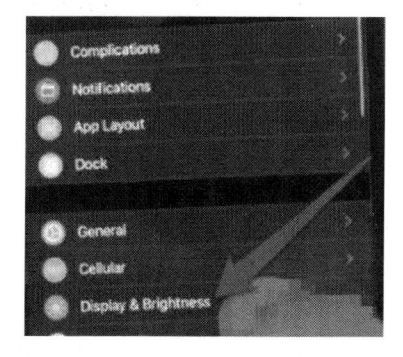

Step 3: tap on *Always On*

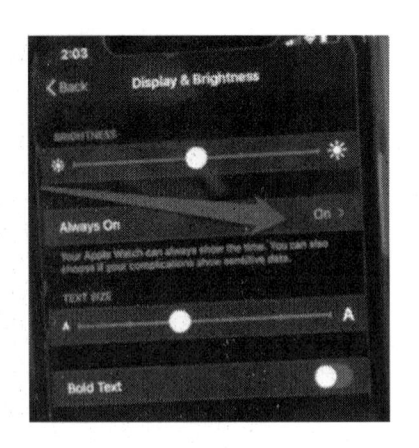

Step 4: Toggle off *Always On*

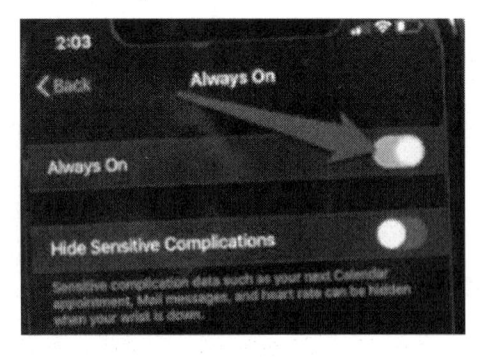

You can also de-activate the *Always-On* feature through the *Settings menu* on your series 5 watch. Simply tap on the settings icon, under *Display and Brightness,* select *Always-on.* You can either choose to activate or deactivate the feature.

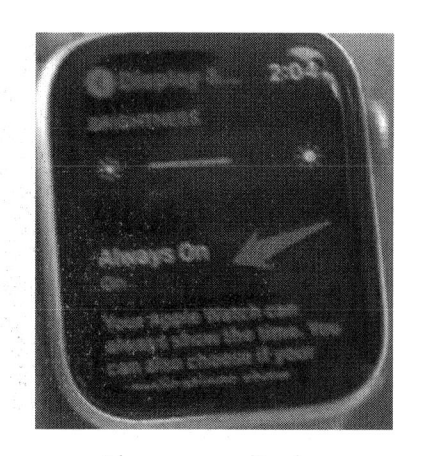

Always on display

How to increase and decrease the brightness of your Apple watch

You can increase or decrease the brightness of your Apple watch series 5 by tapping on the *Settings icon* on your watch. Next, under *Display and Brightness,* locate the *Brightness* icons, tap on the right icon to increase the brightness, and on the left icon to reduce it.

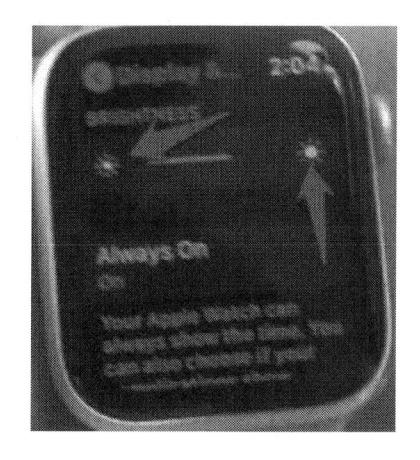

Increase and decrease brightness level

How to change text size

Go to the settings menu on your watch. Next, scroll down and select *Text Size*. You can either increase or decrease the text size by tapping on the **Aa** icon to the left or the right of your watch's screen.

Increase or decrease text size

How to use the compass

The apple watch series 5 comes with an amazing pre-installed compass which displays the accurate direction you're headed. Whenever you activate the app on your watch, it displays the accurate co-ordinates of your position in North, North-East, North- West, South, South- East or South-West.

To use the compass app, select the compass app on your watch, it immediately displays the exact direction you are.

Series 5 compass

How to get notification of the time every 15 minutes, 30 minutes or 1 hour

Do you know that you can always set your watch to notify you of the time at intervals of 15 minutes, 30 minutes or 1 hour? This makes it incredibly easier for you to time things. To achieve this, simply go to your *phone settings*, select *accessibility,* next, select *Chimes,* then choose *Schedule* and select your preferred notification interval.

The steps are graphically illustrated below:

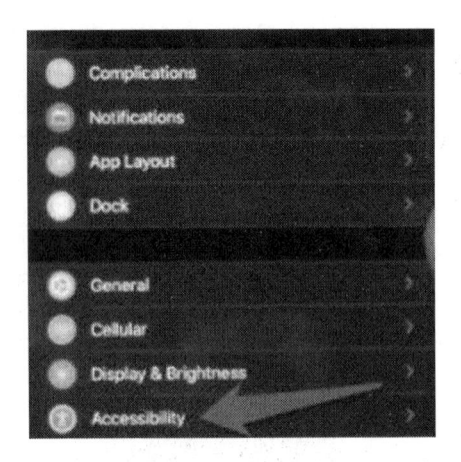

From *Settings*, select *Accessibility*

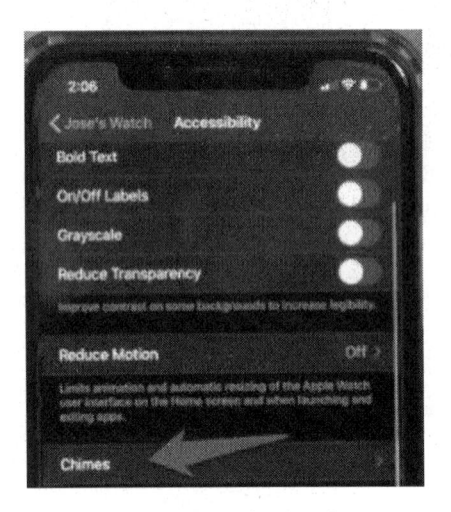

Next, select *Chimes*

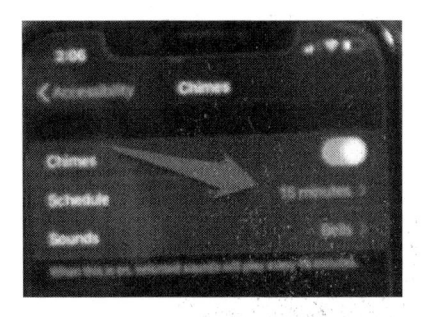

Select *Schedule*

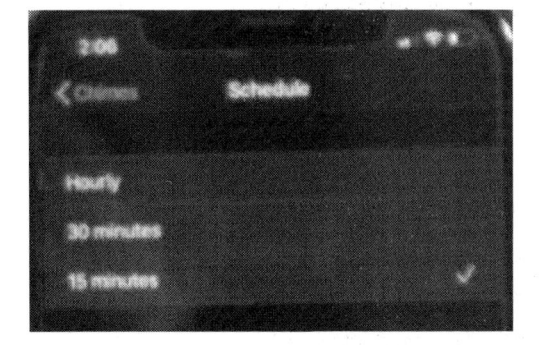

Choose your preferred time interval

How to use fall detection

The fall detection feature is especially useful for the elderly and those who work in a dangerous or hazardous environment, prone to the risk of tripping and falling. Your watch can call an emergency contact on your emergency contact list whenever it detects a hard fall and did not get any response from you. This feature can save one from dangerous situations.

To activate this feature, scroll through your watch app settings menu on your phone and select *Emergency SOS*. Next, toggle on *Fall detection*.

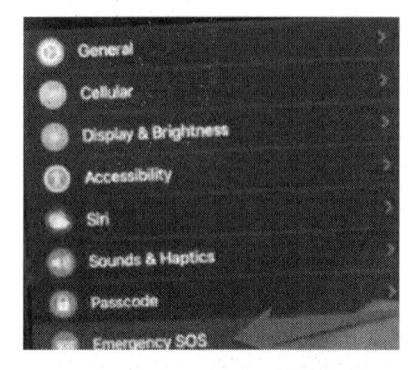

Select *Emergency SOS*

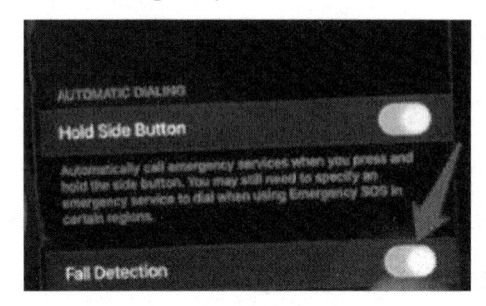

Toggle on *Fall Detection*

How to delete apps

To delete any unwanted app on your series 5 watch, press down on the app until you see a little 'x' icon on the top edge of the app. Tap on the 'x' icon and you will find an option to delete.

Long press on the app you want to delete   select *Delete App*

How to quickly mute your series 5 watch by covering with your palm

You can quickly prevent your watch from making any notification sounds, whenever you are in a meeting or when you just do not want to be disturbed. You can do this by using your palm to cover the screen of your phone for at least 3 seconds. To achieve this, open the watch app on your phone, scroll down and select *Sounds and Haptics*. Next, toggle on the *Cover to mute* option.

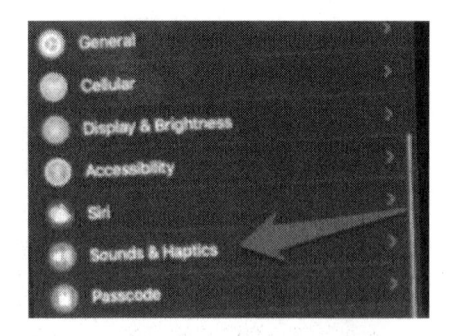

Select *Sounds & Haptics*

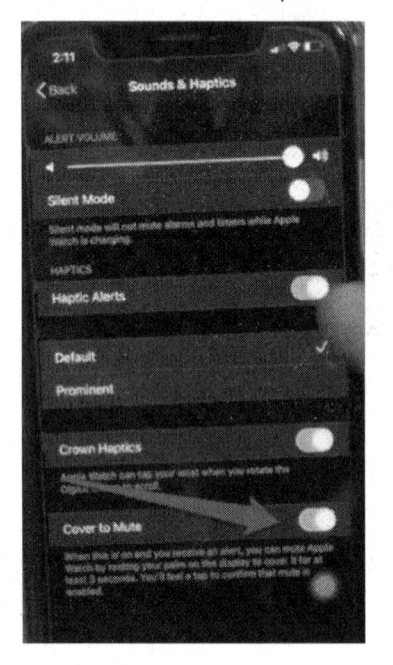

Activate the *Cover to Mute* option

Hear your watch speak the time

You can hear your watch speak the time by tapping its screen with two fingers.

33

The Calculator

You can now assess the calculator on your watch. The calculator is one of the new features introduced to the Apple watch series 5. One of the hidden features in the calculator is the *Tip*. You can now easily calculate tips on your watch.

Calculator app 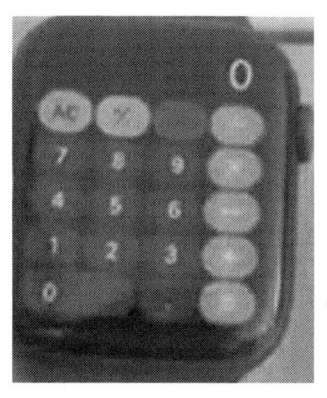   calculator features

Calculator *Tip* feature

How to ascertain the stability of any object

You can determine the stability of an object by placing your watch on the object. When you place your watch on the object, it tells you the level of inclination. This is another amazing feature of the compass. Launch the compass app on your watch and scroll down using the digital crown and place your watch on your desired object to get the accurate level of inclination and ground elevation.

Rotate the digital crown   Shows inclination and elevation

How to automatically unlock your watch with your iPhone

You can unlock your apple watch series 5 with your iPhone. This means that whenever you unlock your iPhone, your watch also gets unlocked. To activate this feature, launch the watch app from your phone, and select *Passcode*. Next, toggle on *Unlock with iPhone* option.

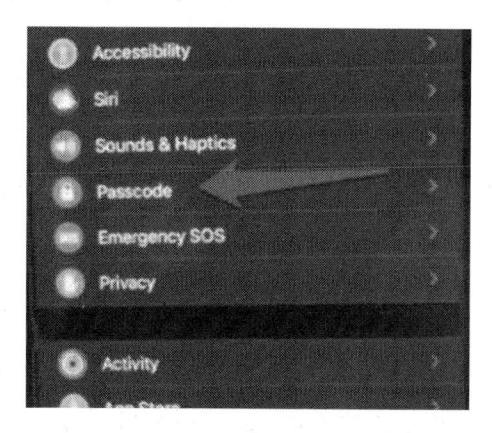

Select Passcode

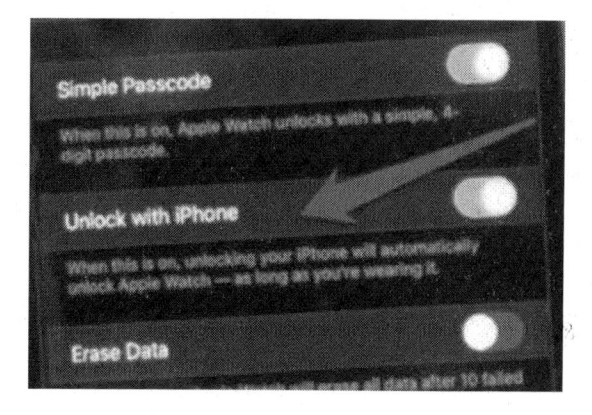

How to find your phone with your Apple watch series 5

You can use your watch to find your phone, if misplaced. Go to the control center of your watch and press the phone icon as shown in the image below. Your phone will then automatically make sounds so that you can easily locate it.

Press the phone icon as indicated by the arrow.

How to take screenshots on your watch

You can take screenshots on your watch by pressing the side button. However, you first have to activate the feature from the settings on your phone. To activate this feature, go to the watch settings on your phone, select *General*. Next, select *Enable Screenshots.*

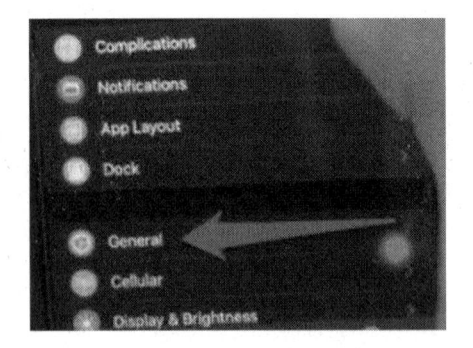

Select *General*

37

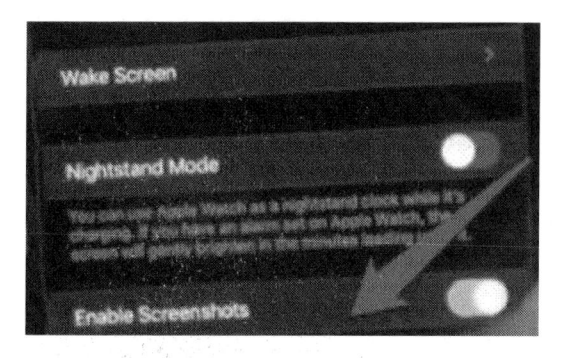

Activate *Enable Screenshots*

How to use voice memos

There is a brand new voice recording app on your apple watch series 5. The voice recording app enables you record and save your voice as a voice memo. All these can be done directly from your apple watch. All you have to do is to tap the record button to start recording voice memos and tap on the stop button when you are done. You can play back and even share your voice memos with your contacts.

Select the voice recording app   Tap the red circle to start recording

Tap on the red square to end recording

How to use the weather app

You can quickly get weather updates on your watch. Simply launch the weather app on your watch and long press to see the percentage of rain, condition of the weather and the temperature outside.

How to re-arrange the layout

You can quickly change the layout of your phone from your watch. Hard press the screen of your watch series 5 and select either *List View* or *Grid View*.

Select either list or grid view to change the layout on your phone

How to find recently opened apps on your Apple watch series 5

Your watch will reveal the recently opened apps when you press the power button. You can also easily remove unwanted apps from your recently opened list by swiping the apps to the left side and tapping the "x" icon.

Measure sound in your area

Another new app is the noise app. The noise app actually allows you to measure sound in your area. By determining how loud the noise is, you can protect your ears and keep away from dangerously loud noises that could damage your hearing.

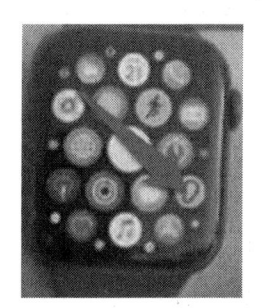

How to change your watch faces

Your apple watch series 5 comes in a variety of faces you can choose from. One of the first things you could when you power your watch is to swipe through to view the different unique faces. These watch faces can also be customized.

You can customize a face by pressing down on a face and tapping the *customize* bar. You can also change the display of your watch by simply swiping its screen to the left or right. As you swipe the screen, different faces get displayed. You can add more faces by first pressing down the watch face and swiping through the faces until you see *New*. Tap on *New* and choose your preferred face. You can also change the display colors and even add some apps for easy access on some of the faces.

How to force restart

Whenever your apple watch freezes, you can easily restart it by pressing down both the crown and power buttons simultaneously. Pressing both buttons at the same time restarts your watch and solves the freezing problem.

How to use the theatre mode

One of the options in the control center is the theatre mode. The theatre mode turns of all notifications when you are in a movie or watching a play.

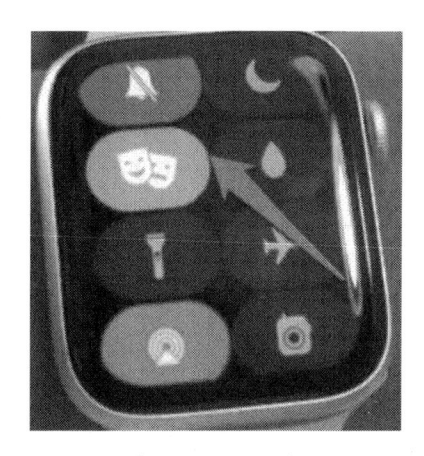

Theatre mode

How to protect your phone from water

The *water lock* is another feature of the control center on your watch, which enables you to swim without having to worry about the screen of your watch. When you activate the *Water lock* mode, the screen of your watch gets locked, preventing water from messing it up. You can unlock the water lock mode by scrolling up the crown by the side of your watch.

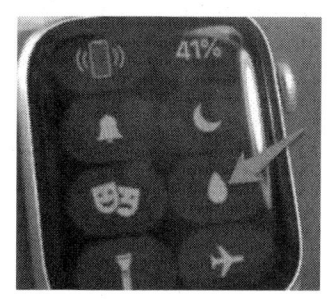

Arrow showing *Water lock* icon

How to add default responses

You can add default responses to notifications on your phone. To achieve this, launch the watch app on your phone. Select *Messages*. Next, select *Default replies* and then type in or enter your choice of default replies.

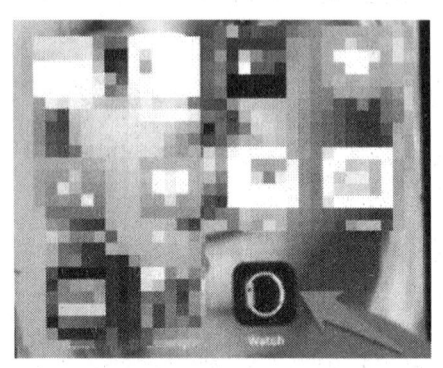

STEP 1: Launch the *Watch app*

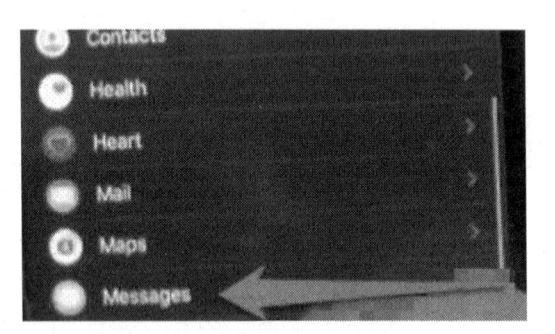

STEP 2: Select *Messages*

43

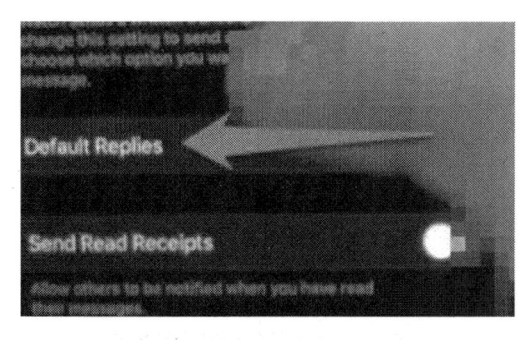

STEP 3: Select *Default Replies*

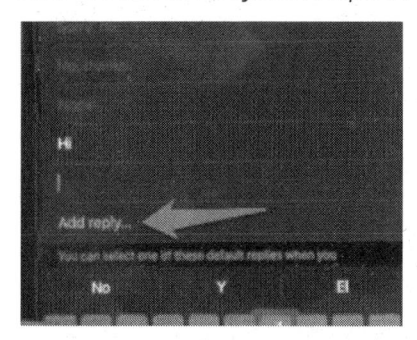

STEP 4: Tap on *Add reply*

How to add contacts to Emergency SOS

You can add several emergency contacts on your apple series 5 watch. To achieve this, launch the watch app on your phone, select *Emergency SOS*. Next, tap on *Edit Emergency Contacts in Medical ID*. Next, fill the required information in *Improve Health & Activity*. Next, select *add emergency contact*. You can then select all the contacts you will like to add to your emergency SOS list.

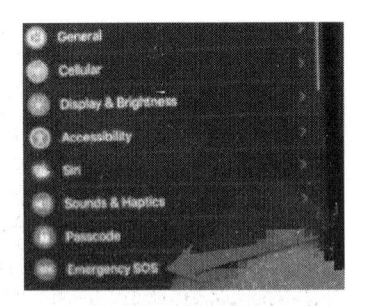

Select *Emergency SOS*

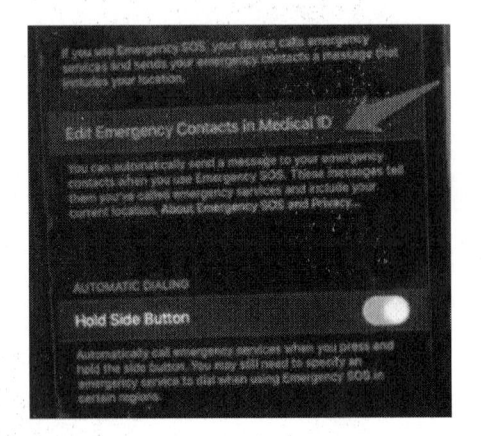

Tap on *Edit Emergency Contacts in Medical ID*

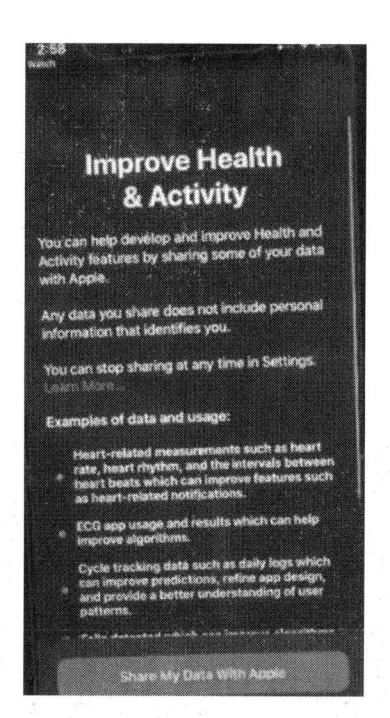

Read the health information

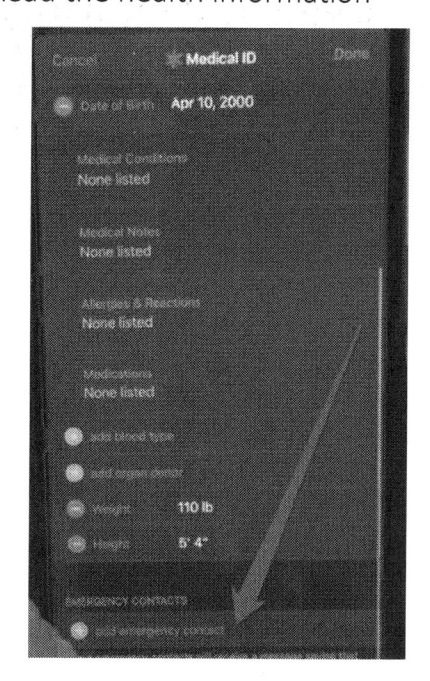

Select *add emergency contact*

How to set a photo as your watch face

You can use any of your photos as your watch face. To achieve this, go to your picture gallery, select any picture of your choice and long press on the picture. Next, tap on *create watch face,* then choose either *photos* or *kaleidoscope*. Setting a photo as your watch face also allows the date and time display.

How to send messages

Sending messages with your watch is super easy. Simply launch the message app on your apple watch series 5 and long press. Next, tap on *New message.* You have a number of options to choose from when sending your messages. You can either choose to send your message via voice note, emoji or writing.

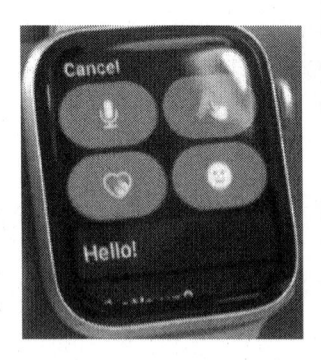

How to customize the control center

To customize the control center, swipe up your watch screen and tap on *Edit*. Next, you can easily move your icons to wherever you want them to be. Tap on *Done* to complete the process.

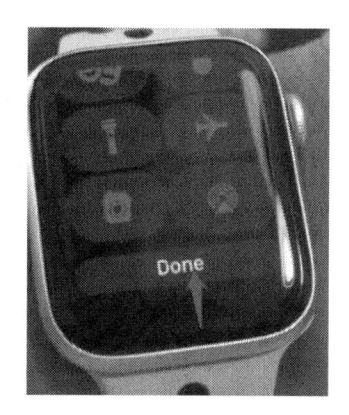

How to use the night stand clock

Your watch can always display the time in *Night mode* whenever you are charging it.

Night mode display

To activate the night mode feature, launch the watch app on your phone. Next, select *General*. Next, toggle on *Night stand mode*.

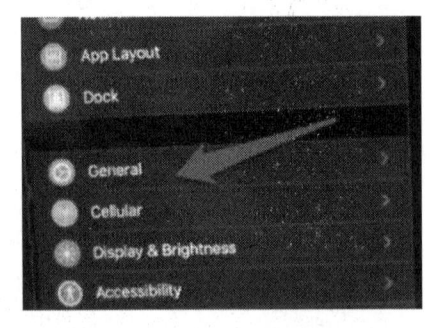

Select *General*

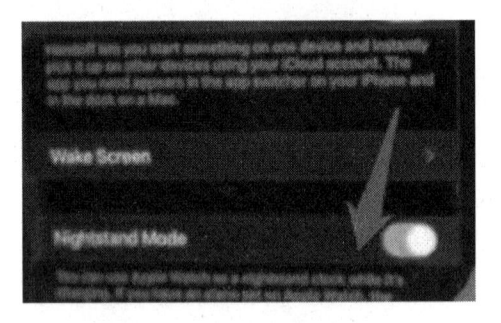

Toggle on *Nightstand Mode*

How to use your apple watch series 5 as a Walkie Talkie

You can connect and talk with your friends apple watch to apple watch. To activate this feature, launch the *Walkie Talkie* app on your watch and select the contact you want to talk to. A notification will be sent to the person.

Walkie Talkie app

How to connect to a Wi-Fi network on your watch

You can connect your watch to a Wi-Fi network without using your phone. To activate this feature, Go to *settings* and select *Wi-Fi*.

Select *Settings*

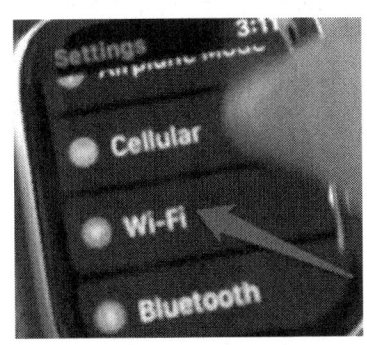

Select *Wi-Fi*

Listen to podcasts on your apple watch

You can listen to podcasts on your apple watch. Simply select podcasts app and wait for it to load completely. Next, select the podcast you would like to listen to.

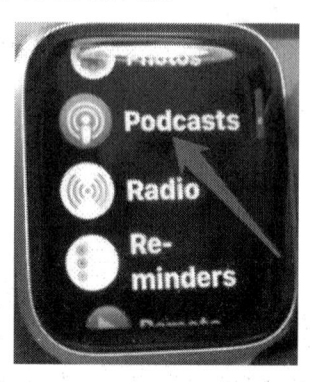

How to turn your apple watch into a flash light

You can turn your apple watch into a flash light, especially for visibility in the dark. When the flash light is activated, the face of your watch becomes a flash light. There are varieties of light colors to choose from.

Flash light icon

How to check your storage capacity

You can check the storage capacity and app usage of your watch. to do this, launch the watch app on your phone. Next, select *General*. Next, select *About*. You would find details about the storage capacity and available space on your watch and many other useful information about your watch.

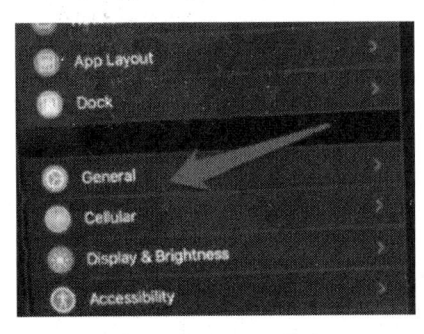

Select *General*

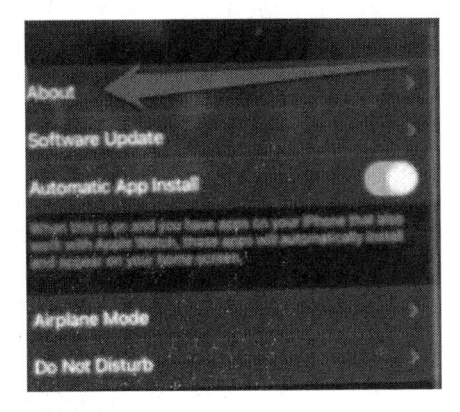

Select *About*

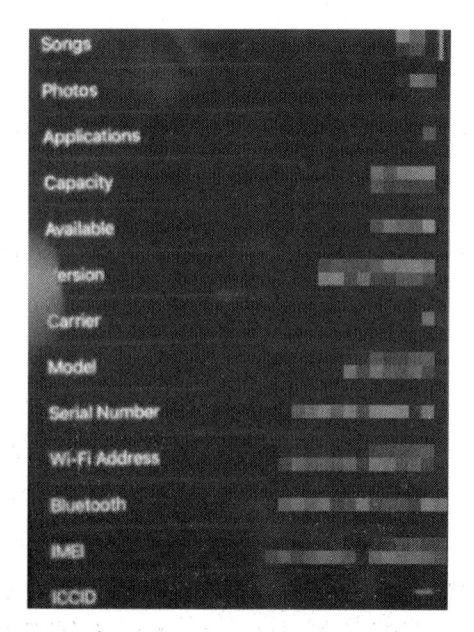

Useful details about your phone

How to place a call on hold

Whenever you receive a call and would like to answer it on your phone, tap on the three dotted icon beside the green answer call icon on your watch. Next, select *Answer on iPhone*. Your call gets automatically placed on hold until you find your iPhone.

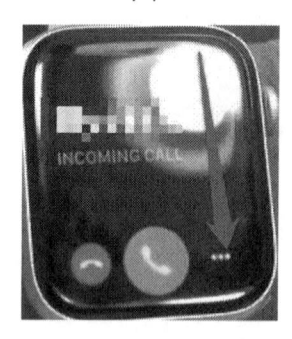

Tap on the three dotted icon

Select *Answer on iPhone*.

How to select apps to get notifications from on your watch

You can customize your notifications by selecting the apps you would like to get notifications from. To achieve this, launch the watch app on your phone and select *Notifications*. Next, select toggle on the apps you would like to get notifications from and off the ones you would not like to get notifications from.

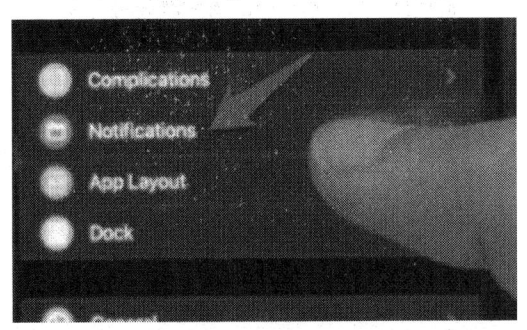

Select *Notifications*.

How to connect your apple watch to your iPhone

To connect your apple watch series 5 to your iPhone, ensure you have an iPhone ios 8.2 or later versions and also have the apple watch application installed on your phone. It should be installed with the latest ios update. Next, go to your apple watch, press and hold the side button, the apple logo will pop up as the watch comes on.

Power on your watch

Next, select your preferred language.

To start pairing, pick up your iPhone and swipe up to access the control center, then turn on your Wi-fi and bluetooth.

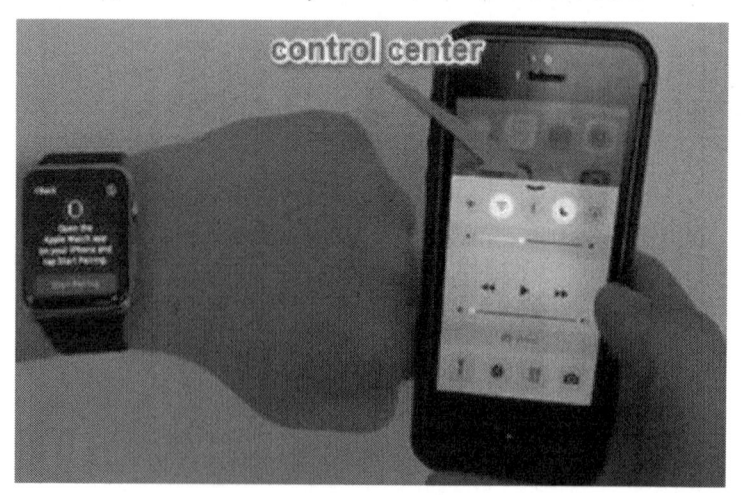

Turn on Wi-fi and bluetooth from the *Control center*

Next, go into the apple watch app on your iPhone and click on *Start pairing*. Also, click on *Start pairing* on your apple watch. Use your phone scan camera to locate your apple watch to pair instantly and easily. Next, click *Set up apple* watch on your iPhone screen. Next, choose the wrist you wear the apple watch. choose either left or right depending on what your preference may be. The apple watch will be calibrated and set up according to your preference. Next, agree to the *terms and conditions*, by clicking *Agree* and then you will be required to enter your *Apple ID password*. Next, select *OK* if you want to turn on location services, siri, and diagnostics.

You can actually add an apple watch passcode from the screen of your phone, but that will require an apple passcode on your apple watch. Next, install available applications. Next, the apple watch starts synching to your iPhone and will notify you when the synchronization process has reached completion.

Chapter 5

Features and Settings

Homescreen

You can access the homescreen of your apple watch by pressing once on the digital crown. To move around the homescreen, you only have to press and move your finger to swipe around. This enables you to see the different applications that are available. To open up an app, you just have to tap once on the app. To go back to the homescreen, press the digital crown once again. To access your recently opened app, just double press the digital crown.

How to view your battery percentage

You can view your battery percentage from the glances menu. The glance menu gives a quick access to different applications. To assess the battery percentage, swipe the homescreen from below, then keep swiping to the left until you get to your battery percentage.

Power reserve

The power reserve feature is great for preserving your battery when it is low. The power reserve option will always display the time, while the other applications will not be available to use. To activate the power reserve mode, all you have to do is to press and hold the power button by the side of your watch, until the options of turning off and power reserve displays on the screen. Swipe the power reserve option to activate it. The power reserve saves a lot of battery power. To deactivate this setting, you have to restart your watch to bring you back to your normal apple watch functionality.

How to customize your watch faces

Your apple watch comes with several beautiful faces which you can either customize, use as they are or create your own. Among the watch faces include: utility, modular, simple, motion, astronomy, color, chronograph, solar, mickey and extra-large.

To customize your watch face, all you have to do is to hold and press the watch face until you see the *customize bar* pop just below the watch face. You can swipe through the screen to view other available watch faces and tap on the *customize bar* to begin customizing your preferred face, or you can decide to creat new watch face by selecting *New*. You can customize details of your watch face with your digital crown. You can customize the color, date display, stopwatch, battery, world clock, weather and many more details. There are so many possibilities with the apple watch.

Notifications

When you have a red dot at the top of your apple watch screen, it means you have unread notifications. The messages are supposed to show instantly on your screen as you receive them, but if you wait for a few minutes and you keep seeing the red dot, just swipe from the top of your screen to view the notifications. Click on the message and decide to either dismiss or reply the message. When you click on reply, it will come up with quick and easy responses based on what it thinks the text is saying, you can also choose to reply with an emoji or even dictate text to siri to reply for you, which can be sent in either audio or text.

Responding to E-mails

E-mails also show up in the notification section.You can click on your mail to read it instantly. Unfortunately you would need to reply to your emails using your phone. When you press and hold. You have the options to flag as important, mark as unread and move to archive.

Answering phone calls

The apple watch allows you to answer calls easily, especially in areas where you cannot easily use your phone.When a call comes in on your apple watch, you can see who is calling. You have the options to either accept the call, reject the call, send a message or answer on your iPhone.

How to transfer calls

To transfer calls from your apple watch to your iPhone is easy, tap the green bar at the top left of your phone and your call will immediately gets transferred to your iPhone.

Tap the green bar to transfer call from your watch to your phone.

Access keypad

Most times, the need to access your keypad while on a call arises. To bring up your keypad while on a call, you have to swipe up on your screen and instantly you will find an option to bring up the keyboard.

Glances

The glances allows you have quick access to different features on your apple watch. the first set of glance features are the airplane mode, do not disturb and the sound settings. You can swipe over and access the music settings, where you can play music saved on your iPhone or those saved directly on your apple watch. you can alsogo forward or backward on your music list, play or pause your music and even increase or decrease your music volume. you also have the heart rate amongst the glance features, the battery percentage, power reserve, the events, weather, stocks, maps, world time and also the activity app.

Alarms, Timers, world clock and stop watch

Alarms

To set up your alarm, launch the alarm icon from the homescreen of your watch. Next, tap and hold firmly to bring up the *New* menu, click on it and draft a brand new alarm. The alarm on your watch works similarly to the alarm on your iPhone.

Timer

To set up your timer application, launch the timer icon from the homescreen of your watch. Next, you can set a timer for your preferred duration by using the digital crown to indicate the time limit. When you start the timer, it keeps counting down even when you exit the timer app. You can also include your timer on the top left of your watch face, by pressing down the watch face and clicking on *customize.* Next, use your digital crown to locate the timer and set the duration you want.

Stop watch

When you open the stop watch app and long press the screen, you would find the different world clock features. They are: Analog, Digital, Graph, and Hybrid. You can explore all the different features of the stop watch app. I personally prefer the Analog view, as it simple to use.

Track health and fitness

One of the main reasons people get an apple watch is to use the health and fitness tracker. To activate the health fitness tracker, swipe up to the glance features and go over to the glance that says *Set up the activity app* and click rght there. You will find a list of activities and their daily goals. The activities include:

Stand: stand for at least one hour

Move: hit your personal calorie burn goal by moving more.

Exercise: accumulate 30 minutes of activity or above a brisk walk

Next, tap *Get started* and then fill out your profile and tap continue. After you complete your set up, you will be able to see your activities on standing, moving and exercising. You can monitor your progress with the apple watch application on your phone as well. You can also customize and add the health tracker to your watch face.

Apple pay and pass book

The apple pay enables you to contactllessly pay for your different purchase at select stores. To set up apple pay and pass book on your apple watch, all you need to do is to go to your my watch app on your iPhone. Next, select *Passbook & Apple Pay*. You can always set up your credit card or mirror your iPhone. You can also add up different credit cards or debit cards. After you're done with the settings on your phone, double tap the power button on your watch to access apple pay.

To access your passbook, go to your homescreen and launch the passbook application where you would find all the different kinds of cards and passes you have in the pass book application.

Maps on the apple watch

In the apple watch map, you can zoom in and zoom out using the digital crown. You can also press and hold to find nearby locations. Or you can use your contacts to find where your friends currently are. You can also use the location settings at the bottom left to find out where you currently are. You can also find directions and send directions over to your iPhone.

Remote control

Remote contorl enables you to instantly control your computer or i tunes and even apple Tv

Stocks

Allows you view the different stocks in your area.

How to download third party app on your watch

Take your iPhone and go over to the apple watch application. You can search for applications or view featured applications. To download, make sure you have purchased the app, then go back to the my watch app category and scroll down until you have found the application you purchased. Select the app and toggle on *show on apple watch*. The app will get directly installed to your apple watch. To delete the downloaded app from your watch, long press on the app until an 'x' icon appears, then tap to delete it. Please, note that the app will still be on your phone after deleting from your watch, so, ensure to also delete from your phone if you no longer need the app. You can also show the downloaded app in *glances* when you toggle on the *show on glances* option

Chapter 6

Siri

Siri is one of the amazing features also present in the Apple watch series 5. To access Siri, long press on the digital crown. When you give a voice command to Siri, you will get a voice or digital feedback through the screen and speaker of your watch. The Apple watch series 5 also enables the conversion of voice note to text.

Basic Siri Commands

Below is a list of Siri commands. Note that this list is not exhaustive, as the listof Siri commands continues to expand with continuous improvement.You can also tweak some of the commands to get similar results.

- **To adjust watch volume**: *"Hey Siri, turn up/down the volume,"* *"Hey Siri, set the volume to 3,"*
- **To request for help**: *"Hey, Siri, help."*
- **To converse with Siri**: *"Hey Siri, let us chat"*
- **To Display Photos**: *"Hey Siri, show me my photos"* or, *"Hey Siri, show me pictures of mountains."*
- **To return your watch to homescreen**: *"Hey Siri, return home."*

- **To display weather forecast:** *"Hey Siri, show me the weather forecast"*
- **To open an app:** *"Hey Siri, open Uber."*
- **To display food recipes:** *"Hey Siri, show me the recipes for salad"*

Time and Date

- **Ask Siri for time:** *"Hey Siri, what time is it?"*
- **Ask Siri for date:** *"Hey Siri, what's today's date?"*
- **Ask Siri to check for dates or events:** *"Hey Siri, when is (holiday) this year?"*
- **Ask Siri to set an alarm:** *"Hey Siri, set an alarm for 1 p.m."* or *"Hey Siri, remind me of my meeting at 3 p.m."*
- **Ask Siri to set a repeating alarm:** *"Hey Siri, set a repeating alarm for Sundays at 5 a.m."*
- **Ask Siri to set a music alarm:** *"Hey Siri, wake me up to(song, playlist, genre, artist, or album)*
- **Ask Siri to set a timer:** *"Hey Siri, set a timer"* or *"Hey Siri, set a timer for 30 minutes."*
- **Ask Siri to create multiple timers:** *"Hey Siri, set a second timer for 8 minutes."*
- **Ask Siri to create a timer with a name:** *"Hey Siri, set a studying timer for 2 hours"*
-

Information search

- **Ask Siri a general question:** *"Hey Siri, when did the United states of America gain independence?"*
- **Get a quote from Game of thrones:** *"Hey, Siri, give me a quote from Game of thrones."*
- **Getting information from wikipedia:** *"Hey Siri, Wikipedia {subject}."*
- **Ask Siri to read a wikipedia entry completely:** *"Hey Siri, tell me more"*

Calculations and Conversions

- **Basic mathematics:** *"Hey Siri, what's 4 divided by 2?"* or *"Hey Siri, what's 4 plus 4?"*

Sports Update

- **Ask when a team's next game is scheduled:** *"Hey Siri, when does the (team) play next?"*
- **Checking the results of a finished game:** *"Hey Siri, what was the score of the (team) game?"*
- **Find out the result of your favorite teams:** *"Hey Siri, give me my sports update"*
- **Ask if a team won a game:** *Hey Siri, did the (team) win.*
- **Get league standing of all teams:** *"Hey Siri, what are the standings of MLB"*

- Get fantasy football update with the yahoo fantasy football skill: *"Hey Siri, ask Yahoo Fantasy For a score update"*

Information on Food and Businesses

- Get the operation hours or contacts of local businesses: *"Hey siri' find business hours for Zerox"*
- Locate a nearby restaurant: *"Hey Siri, find me the nearest liquor bar"*
- Get food recipes: *"Hey Siri, how do you make pasta."*

Accurate Definitions And Spellings

- Get the correct spelling of a word: *"Hey Siri, how do you spell (word)?"*
- Get the definition of a word: *"Hey Siri, what is the definition of (word)?"*

Set Up To-do and Shopping Lists

- Check shopping list: *"Hey Siri, what's on my shopping list?"*
- Create your shopping list: *"Hey Siri, I will be buying a crate of eggs"* or *" Hey Siri, add bread to my shopping list."*
- Create a reminder: *"Hey Siri, remind me to visit the doctor in 20 minutes."*
- Check existing reminders: *"Hey Siri, what are my reminders for today?"* or *"what reminders do I have today?"*
- Check events on a calendar: *"Hey Siri, what's on my calendar for this weekend?"*

- **Add events to your calendar:** *"Hey Siri, add an event to my calendar"* or *"Hey Siri, add (event) to my calendar for (day) at (time)."*
- **Add task to your to-do list:** *"Hey Siri, I need to make an appointment with the Priest"* or *"Hey Siri, add "study" to my to-do list."*

Entertainment Updates

- **To get information on movies playing:** *"Hey Siri, tell me about the movie (title)."*
- **To get IMDb rating:** *"Hey, Siri, what is the IMDb rating for (movie or TV show)."*
- **To search for movies at a nearby cinema:** *"Hey Siri, what movies are showing now?"*
- **To get cast for a movie:** *"Hey Siri, who plays in (movie title)?"*
- **Find out an actor's latest work:** *"Hey Siri, what is (actor)'s latest movie?"*
- **Find out the name of a musician who sang the song playing on your device or at random:** *"Hey Siri, who sang the song (title)?"*
- **Find popular music by an artist:** *"Hey Siri, what's popular from (artist)?"*
- **Find an album or song:** *"Hey Siri, find (album or song) by (artist)*

- **Find the names of musical band members:** *"Hey Siri, who is in the band (name)?"*
- **Show available seasons of movies:** *"Hey Siri, show me seasons of (movie title)*

Media Controls

- **Command Siri to play music:** *"Hey Siri, play some music."*
- **Command Siri to play song based on content:** *"Hey Siri, play the latest Beyonce's album." Or "Hey Siri, play the song with lyrics 'Baby I can feel you tonight.'"*
- **Command Siri to place specific song or artist on a queue:** *"Hey Siri, play music by (artist)."*
- **Play music based on a theme:** *"Hey Siri, play me some POP music" or "Hey Siri, play me some gospel music."*
- **Replay a song:** *"Hey Siri, replay."*
- **Command Siri to set a timer for sleep:** *"Hey Siri, set a sleep timer for 1 hour" or "Hey Siri, stop playing in 30 minutes"*
- **Command Siri to control music:** *"Hey Siri, next" or "Hey Siri, play"*

Holidays

- **Get information about a holiday:** *"Hey Siri, why do we celebrate (holiday)?"*
- **Know when a holiday is coming up:** *"Hey Siri, when is (holiday)?"*

- **Ask Siri to sing a christmas carol**: *"Hey Siri, sing a Christmas carol"*
- **Ask Siri to track Santa**: *"Hey Siri, where is Santa"* or *"Hey Siri, track Santa"*
- **Ask Siri about Santa:** *"Hey Siri, how old is Santa Claus?"* or *"Hey Siri, where does Santa Claus come from?"* or *"Hey Siri, is Santa Claus real?"*
- **Spin the dreidel**: *"Hey Siri, spin the dreidel."*
- **Ask Siri about a Holiday limerick:** *"Hey Siri, tell me a holiday limerick"*
- **Get information about holiday movies:** *"Hey Siri, What's your favorite holiday movie?"* or *"Hey Siri, what are the top movies this holiday"*
- **Ask Siri for Holiday jokes**: *"Hey Siri, how ugly is your/my night gown"* or *"Hey Siri, tell me a night time joke"*
- **Have Siri read 'the night before Christmas':** *"Hey Siri, read "The Night Before Christmas."*
- **Ask about Santa's reindeer:** *"Hey Siri, what do you know about Santa's reindeer?"* or *"Hey Siri, who's your favorite reindeer"* or *"Hey Siri, what do you know about Rudolph the rednoseed reindeer?"*

News and Weather Update

- **Get weather updates:** *"Hey Siri, what's the weather like today?"* or *"Hey Siri, will it be cloudy today?"* or *"Hey Siri, will I need to go out with an umbrella today?"*
- **Get News headlines:** *"Hey Siri, what's in the news today"*
- **Ask for weather forecast:** *"Hey Siri, what's the weather going to look like tomorrow?"*
- **Ask for updates on traffic situation:** *"Hey Siri, what's traffic like today?"*

Chapter 7

Master The Electrocardiodiagram (ECG) on Apple Watch Series 5

Set Up the ECG App

This section will cover all you need to know about the Electrocardiogram (ECG) feature on the Apple watch 5. However, the information in this chapter should not replace an experts advice on the subject matter. Whenever you have health issues, ensure you consult your doctor for a proper medical check up.

What is Electrocardiogram? The Electrocardiogram still remains one of the most popular featuures on the apple watch.

Electrocardiogram simply means the measurement of electrical activity of the heart. In 1903, Willem Einthoven, a Dutch doctor, invented the first pactical Electrocardiogram.
.

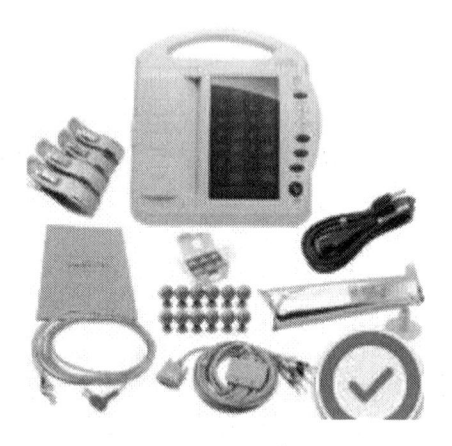

An ECG machine

To aid your understanding on how the AApple watch ECG works, it is important to first understand how the traditional ECG works. The components that make up an ECG machine include ten electrodes, which also have twelve separate vectors. The function of the vectors is to provide all the necessary information to look at the heart's activity.

To set up the ECG on your apple watch 5, launch the ECG app on your watch homescreen. Next, gsearch for the ECG app on your phone and launch it.

The conduction system of the heart

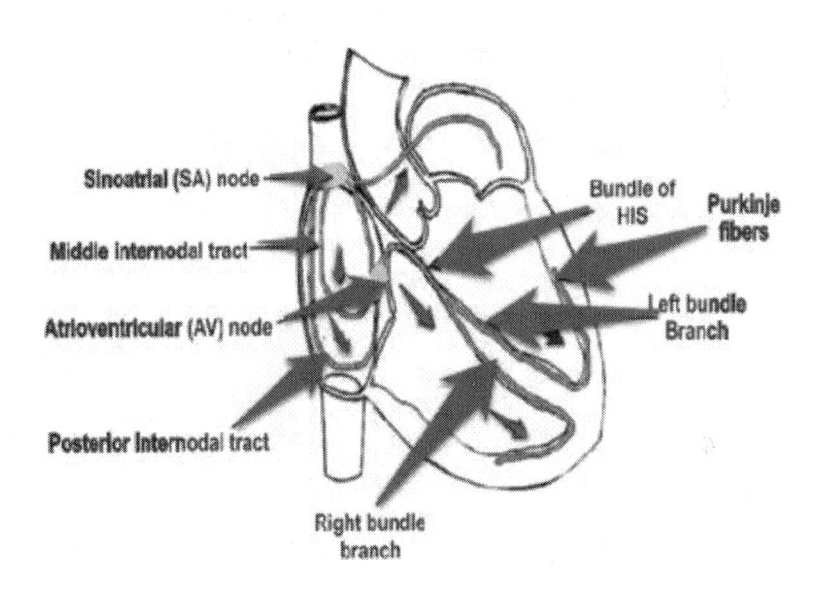

- Sinoatrial (SA) node
- Middle internodal tract
- Atrioventricular (AV) node
- Posterior internodal tract
- Bundle of HIS
- Purkinje fibers
- Left bundle Branch
- Right bundle branch

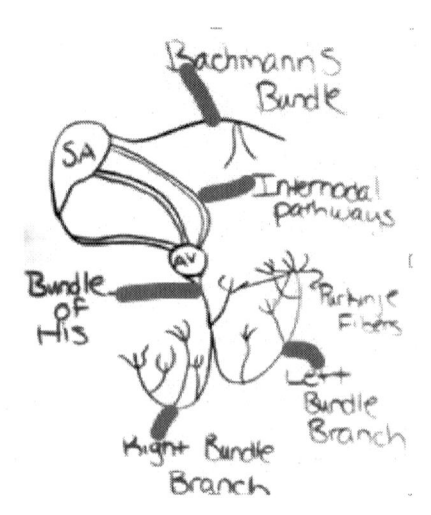

Showing the electrical pathway of the heart

The process by which electrical signals pass through the heart is referred to as the *Conduction system*. The portion of the right atrium, which consists of a group of cells, is where electrical signals begin in the heart. This right atrium is called the Sinoatrial(SA) node. The cells generate an action potential without any nervous input of about 75 beats per minute. Though, these cells are found at the right atrium, yet, they penetrate the wall between the right and left atrium.

Whenever blood squeezes down the ventricles, it is most likely that the movement of electric signals has led to the depolarization of the entire atrium, which usually results in the mechanical contraction of the atria.

Another group of cells are also present in the right atrium; these group of cells is called atrioventricular (AV) nodes. You can find these cells at the bottom of the atria and the top of the ventricles. Signals get transmitted from the SA node to the AV node. The AV node usually generates its action potential between 40- 60 beats per-minute. There is less control of external force, making it slower than the SA mode. There also includes another group of cells known as the AV bundle. The AV bundle is also called the bundle of HIS, which can be found at the top of the interventricular septum (IVS). The AV bundle branches into the left and right bundle branches, sending the bioelectrical signals through the interventricular septum, to depolarize the right and left and ventricles. The left and right bundles extend to the apex part of the heart, where they are referred to as the Purkinje fibers. The right and left ventricles receive signals from the Purkinje fibers. The top of the ventricles is usually the last part of the heart to contract and depolarize. When the atria and the ventricles contract from the bottom, blood is squeezed up and out.

The Apple watch series 5 ECG

The Apple watch series 5 comes with a fantastic ECG feature, which is a read-one ECG. It has two electrodes. The first electrode is the ceramic back at the body of your watch, while the second electrode is the crown which you touch with the finger of your opposite hand. The read- one of the apple watch ECG is highly effective, as it measures the heart rhythm and effectively detects arterial fibrillation. The ECG function of your watch begins to function when your finger is touching the digital crown, and you ask your apple watch to do the ECG. You can also get a prompt. The ECG prompts you using the optical sensor at the back of the watch. Your heart rate gets detected with Photo-plethysmography(PPG). Whenever the apple watch detects you have an irregular heart rate, you will be prompted to perform an ECG. The apple watch looks out for the regularity or irregularity of the p wave. The ECG with arterial fibrillation has an irregular signal without a P wave, while the ECG of a normal heart has a regular P wave. In some instances, arterial fibrillation can be dangerous, while some cases do not pose a threat. For example, a patient could be suffering from low blood pressure (hypotension), where the rest of his body is not getting oxygenated blood. This can also occur when your heart begins to beat faster than usual. This problem is known as Tachycardiac i.e., fast heart rate. When arterial fibrillation is sustained, the chances for cardiac arrest get increased, as well as the risk of stroke.

One of the significant challenges of the apple watch ECG stems from the fact that it only detects arterial fibrillation.

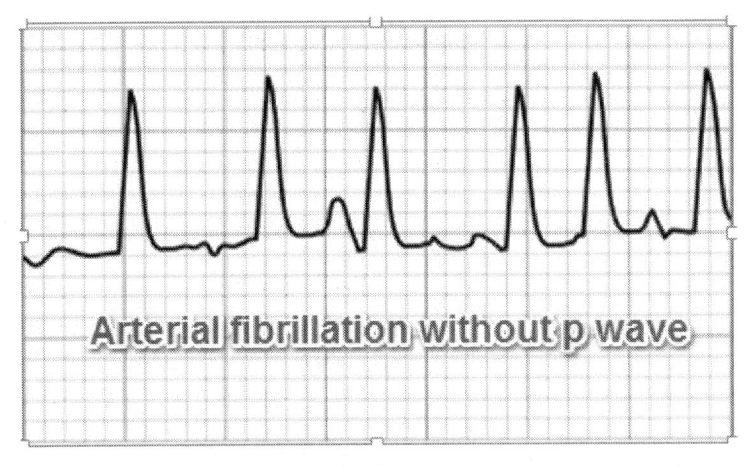

ECG with arterial fibrillation (without p wave)

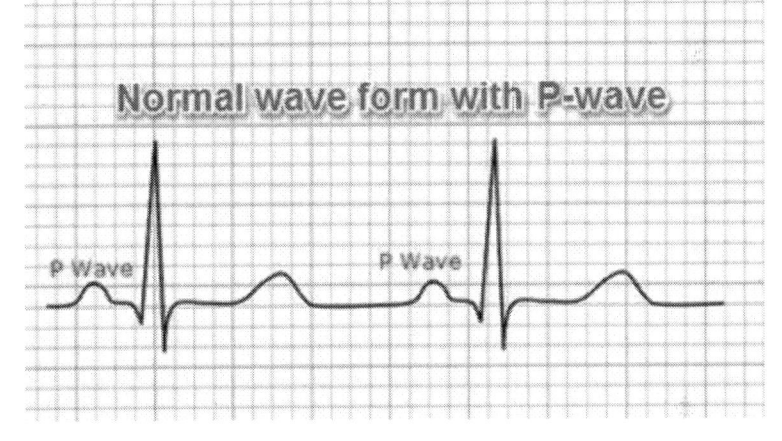

Normal wave form with p wave

Chapter 8

Trouble shooting Apple watch series 5

When your watch gets stuck on the Apple logo

One of the common issues experienced with the apple watch is the watch getting stuck on the Apple logo. To fix this problem, press and hold the digital crown for about 8- 10 seconds. This will restart your apple watch. although, it may take a few minutes.

Tracking problem with GPS location when working out

To improve the GPS location services on your Apple watch, follow these simple steps:

Go to the settings menu on your iPhone. next, scroll down to *Privacy* and tap on *Location services*. Next, check if your Apple watch can use location services and ensure it is turned on while using. NEXT, scroll down to *System services* and ensure that *Motion calibration and distance* is turned on. Next, go to your watch, tap on *Outdoor run* and wait till it completes its three seconds countdown. Swipe to pause the watch. swipe from the bottom to reveal the settings of the watch, if you find a grey arrow at the top right corner of the settings screen, it indicates that your watch has GPS lock. When you find the GPS lock, you are good to go. You can reset, if the GPS calibration is not accurate. Go to your watch app on your phone and select *privacy*. Next, select *Reset fitness calibration*.

When activity does not track accurately

When an activity does not track accurately, you can easily fix this problem with your iPhone and Apple watch.To fix this problem, open settings on your Iphone.Next, tap on *Privacy*. Next, tap on *Location services*. Ensure you turn them *On*. Next, scroll down and tap on *System services*. Turn on *Motion, Calibration and Distance*. Take an outdoor walk for about 15-20 minutes, with your phone and watch. your watch will get calibrated to your movement where you will have more accurate tracking of data. If after doing this you still experience tracking issues, then, launch the Apple watch app on your phone and tap on *Privacy*. Next, tap on *Reset fitness calibration data*. This will wipe out all the stored calibration data you have on your on the watch. Next, take another 20 minute walk, this should fix whatever tracking issues you are experiencing.

When Apple watch does not connect in a cellular way from the iPhone

To solve the problem when your watch does not connect to your iPhone, ensure that your Apple watch and iPhone are up to date on software releases. Next, press down the digital crown and side simultaneously to reset your watch. Resetting your watch will re-establish the cellular connection of your watch.

When you do not receive a feedback from Siri

When you do not receive any feedback from Siri, turn Off the Bluetooth from the setting and turn On the Wi-Fi on your phone. Check if your Apple watch remains connected. Next, go to the control panel on your Apple watch and ensure the Wi-Fi icon is activated. Next, go to *General* and tap on *Siri*. Next, scroll down and select *Siri voice* and wait for it to download.

When the Walkie Talkie is not working

First off, ensure that you have the Face time app on your iPhone. Note that the Walkie Talkie app will not be available on your watch if you have deleted the face time app on your iPhone. The Walkie Talkie app relies strongly on face time audio technology, making it easy for the issue to be fixed through your face time settings. Also, check and ensure Apple ID is set up to use Face time and ensure you can be reached on Facetime on your Apple Id emails and phone number.

One of the frequently encountered problems with Walkie Talkie is using the same Apple ID on different iPhones. When you share same Apple ID with others, your iPhone's walkie talkie will not work.

Sending invitations with the walkie talkie app can also pose a problem. If you encounter any issues relating to sending invitations or getting stocked on the walkie talkie app, remove the contact in the walkie talkie app and resend invitation. You can also try toggling availability *On* and *Off* . Close and re open the app if problem persists.

When you cannot get notifications for messages and E-mails

When you do not get notifications, go to the Apple watch on your iPhone. Next, tap on *Notifications*. Next, tap on *Mail* and select *Mirror my iPhone*. If the issue does not get resolved, tap on *Custom* and toggle on *Show alerts*. Also, go to your *Messages,* tap on *Custom* and toggle on *Show Alerts and Haptic.*

Alternatively, you can fix this problem by going to *Settings* on your iPhone and tap on *Notifications,* ensure you turn on the following: *Allow Notifications, Badge App Icon,* and *Show on Lock screen.*

Repeat the same process for your *Messages*. Following the steps should fix your notification problems.

Chapter 9

Essential Apps for Apple Watch Series 5

Dark sky

The *Dark Sky app* is one of my favorite weather apps you can download on your watch. You can always get up to date information and also find all the weather conditions within the next 24 hours, even down to your pinpoint location. You can choose your work or home address to see what the weather is going to be like at any given time.

Dark sky

Mint

This app allows you to keep track of all of your bank accounts current cash. You will be able to see all the cash and credit debts that you have. You can also see when your bills are due, as well as, check your credit score as well. You can have all of your financial data on your wrist.

1password

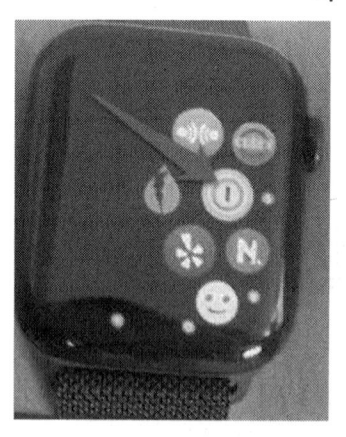

1password app

This app allows you to access all of your passwords on Apple watch with just one password. You can easily log in whenever you are browsing your favourite websites and you want to log in quickly.

Yelp

This is an amazing app that allows you find some of the best restaurants and local businesses in your area, directly from your wristwatch.

Yelp app

Facebook Messenger app

The Facebook Messenger app allows you read your Facebook messages from your watch.

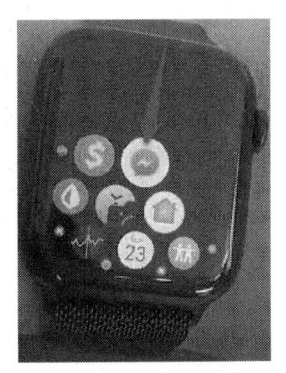

Facebook messenger app

Acorns

This app serves as an interface to co-ordinate your retirement accounts, index funds, trading accounts and also provides several avenues to diversify your index funds and trade on several stocks instead of just trading on only one stock. It is amazing how you can watch your port folio go up. You can also deposit some quick cash without having to open the app always. This is definitely a good means of having some of your spare cash saved.

Starbox App

Starbox fans can install this app to enable them keep track of their points and manage payment.

Shazam

Whenever you are listening to a song and you don't know what it is, the shazam app can tell all about it the song so that you can play it later.

Shazam app

Uber

The uber is a great app on your appple watch. You can make an order and manage it right from your Apple watch.

Uber app

iTranslate Converse App

This app is much needed if you travel a lot. It basically enables the translation from one language to another and it has a whole lot of different languages in store. You can ask any question of your choice, then listen as the watch automatically translates and replies in the language you want it to translate to.

Currency conversion App

This app shows you the current currency rate wherever you are in the world.

In flight

This app is going to allow you to track all your latest flight details. Helping you not to lose your flight.

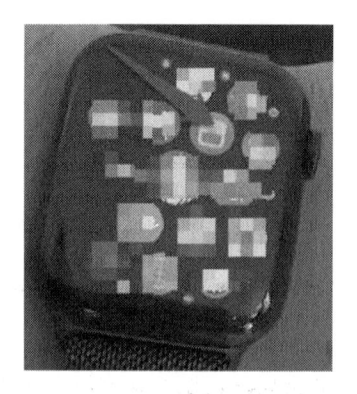

In flight app

Streaks

The Streaks app allows you to have better and smarter habits. Your streaks get tracked everyday as you complete any of the activities on the app. This app is perfectly designed for your Apple watch. when you launch the app, you will find a number of icons, tap on any of them to help you in maintaining a healthy streak. There are several amazing variety of streaks you can engage in to build better, smarter and healthier habits.

Streaks app

My fitness pal

Helps you keep tabs on your calories, carbs, fat and protein intake throughout the day. You can also scroll over to the next page and add water as you drink it to achieve your daily recommended hydration.

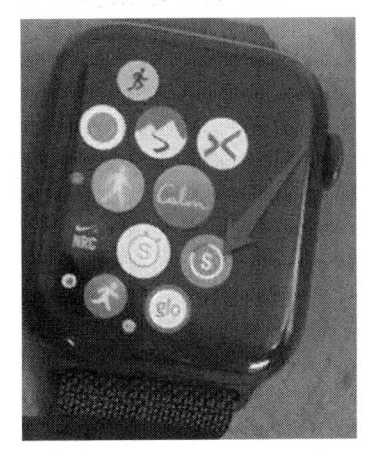

My fitness pal

Headspace

The Headspace app is an amazing app for meditation. You can use this app for quick and effective meditations. It also has an Emergency SOS function which becomes useful in situations where you are stressed out or feeling down.

Audible

Get and listen to audiobooks directly from your Apple watch with this app. You could stream and listen on your ear pods or listen on your watch.

Slope

This app syncs with the Apple watch Health app to monitor calories burnt and report workouts. It also enables you to track skiing when you go down the slope.

Seven

This app is a seven minute work app with lots of amazing features. The workout session lasts for seven minutes. Select a work out session of your choice and follow the procedures.

AutoSleep

You should download this app if you are interested in tracking your sleeping pattern. You can monitor how deep you sleep and the best time for you to wake up.

Calm

This app enables you to play calming sounds directly from your Apple watch, without necessarily going to your iPhone.

YogaGlo

Lovers of yoga can download this great app for doing some Yoga exercises from the Apple Watch.

Bible

You can also download the Bible App on your Apple Watch to read verse of the day and all other trending verses

Podcast player

This is a great app that enables you listen to any of your favourite podcasts

TuneIn

With the TuneIn app, you do not only listen to the radio stations, but also, you get updates on sports radio broadcast. Even when you do not have the time to watch sports on TV, the sports radio broadcast gets you covered.

MyScore

You get up to date information about your favourite sports team and their scores from this app.

Nike Run Club

The Nike Run Club app is great for tracking your exercises. It is similar to *My fitness pal* app

Sworkit

This app comes with several workout rudiments you can choose from.

iHeartRadio

You can listen to thousands of radio stations from anywhere around the world on this app.

Sports App

ESPN

This app enables you to track all the scores and local games playing. To track the games playing, you will need to sync the ESPN to your iPhone.

Fun and Game Apps

Zombies run

This app is a fusion of Health and Fitness app and the fun app. You catch so much fun using the app. When you go omn missions, like running and you plug your earpods into your ear, you can hear what seems like zombies getting closer to you . this makes you want to run faster. Stories about a mission to save people who have been over run by zombies, also motivates you to put in the required effort on your activities.

Runeblade

The runesblade is an amazing game where all you have to do is tap in order to launch an attack. You can customize your characters and your weapons in so many ways. You get to determine how much damage to inflict, increase the attacks or basically how much time your attack will last.

Clockwise

This game app enables players to match different patterns. It is a memory style game where players unveil the patterns and memorize what pops up, then get to locate exactly where they are.

Egg

This game engages you emotionally. You would be required to care for your creature from egg level until when they are hatched.

Rules

This is a game with a set of rules. It is a puzzle you have to solve by following some laid down rules. It is a must have game if you love puzzles.

Lifeline

This game app is text based. You receive a message from a stranded person, requesting your help and you are the only one able to save them. This is a unique game you definitely would like to play many times.

Pokemon Go

All Pokemon Go fans should hurriedly download this amazing app on their Apple watch. In this app you can track down Pokemon wherever they are hiding in your city or town.

Bubblegum Hero

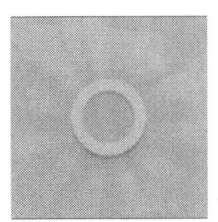

The Bubblegum Hero is an interesting but quite challenging game. In this game, you would be required to press and hold in order to match the size of the bubble you are trying to blow.

Made in the USA
Middletown, DE
24 July 2020